C1

Do not cut out
space between
arm and body.

C

TOM TIERNEY

Cher
Silkwood (1983)

The Witches of Eastwick (1987)

Plate 1

C2

C

Do not cut out
spaces between
arms and bodies.

C

Moonstruck (1987)

Mermaids (1990)

Plate 2

Geena Davis
Thelma and Louise
(1991)

Beetlejuice (1988)

Plate 3

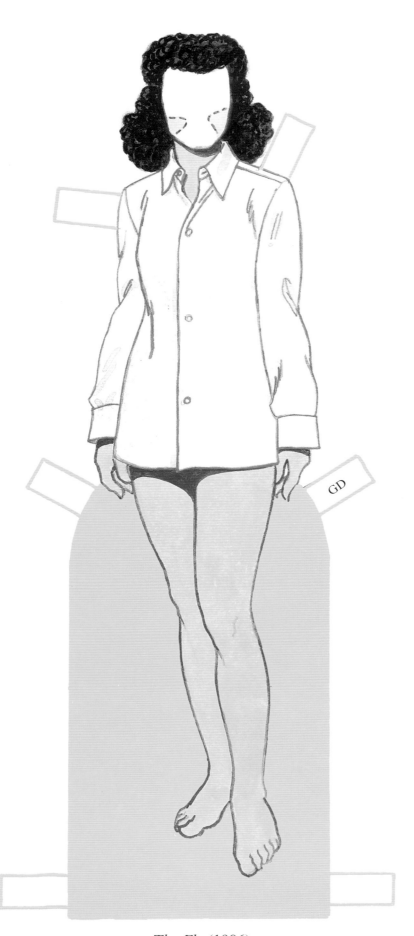

The Fly (1986)

The Accidental Tourist (1988)

Plate 4

GC

GC

Glenn Close
Fatal Attraction (1987)

The Big Chill (1983)

Plate 5

Do not cut out
spaces between
arms and body.

GC

GC

The Natural (1984)

Dangerous Liaisons (1988)

Plate 6

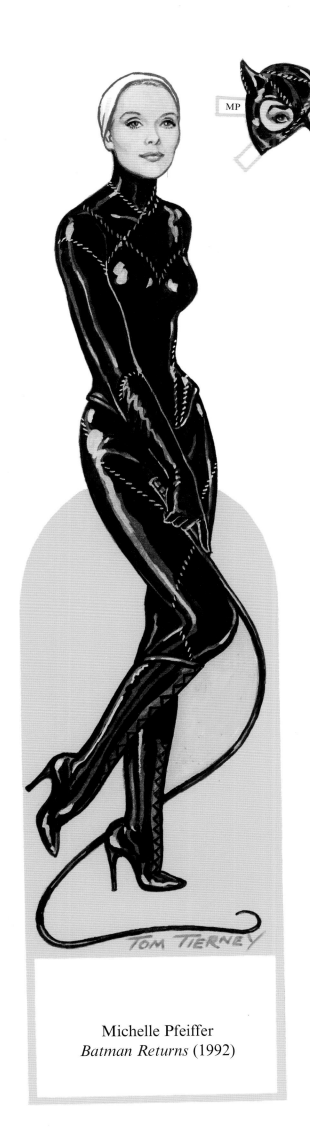

Michelle Pfeiffer
Batman Returns (1992)

Ladyhawke (1985)

Plate 7

Dangerous Liaisons (1988)

The Fabulous Baker Boys (1989)

Plate 8

DP9

DP9

Do not cut out
spaces between
arms and body.

DP

Dolly Parton
Straight Talk (1992)

*The Best Little Whorehouse
in Texas* (1982)

Plate 9

Do not cut out spaces between arms and body.

Steel Magnolias (1989)　　　　　*Nine to Five* (1980)

Plate 10

DH11

DH

Daryl Hannah
Blade Runner (1982)

Steel Magnolias (1989)

Tom Tierney

Plate 11

DH

DH

Do not cut out
space between
arm and body.

The Clan of the Cave Bear (1986)

Splash (1984)

Plate 12

Jessica Lange
The Postman Always Rings Twice
(1981)

TOM TIERNEY

Tootsie (1982)

Plate 13

Do not cut out
spaces between
arms and body.

JL

JL

Sweet Dreams (1985)

Frances (1982)

Plate 14

Bette Midler
Ruthless People (1986)

The Rose (1979)

BM

Plate 15

Outrageous Fortune (1987)

Jinxed! (1982)

Plate 16